GREER SOMMER

An Infinite Web

TOGETHER WE EXIST

Inquiries and Book Orders should be addressed to:

Great Writers Media
Email: info@greatwritersmedia.com
Phone: (302) 918-5570

ISBN: 978-1-960605-79-5 (sc)
ISBN: 978-1-960605-80-1 (ebk)

Dedication

I'm not sure who this book is written for
or whom it may benefit. It might be me,
or you, or someone curious about what's
on the other side? It's confusing to me
as well. I was directed to write. Maybe
not this particular read, but, It was so.

Maybe next time, it will make more sense.
This is true and raw, a fresh abrasion
that raked my leg, leaving remnants of
asphalt embossed. My pulse beats through
my blouse at an accelerated rate.

Welcome to my thoughts and big emotions.
That's mainly when I write, even way back
when. This page, the one I am scribbling
on, a silky, smooth, stark, blank canvas,
an empty vessel, along with a field full
of brilliantly bright and enormous farm

flowers. Encouraging a flow of a .05 ink action, taking me away, like running through rows of Zinnias, Dahlias, and Black-eyed Susans, skipping school during lunch, across the road, at Knott's Berry Farm.

Writing, a place to end rumination and kidnap anxiety, a space to document devastation and delight. And, I am lost in the absorption of ink, despite a minimally toothed page. I'm lost in content, out of the aches, transformed and transitioned like a toxic chemical safely transported, contained, in a warehouse storage space, on an appropriate hazmat shelf, for a different day.

This book is dedicated to my Divine Creator and my children, Lottie, Romy, and my G-d son Rozay: <3 Be Brave, Be Beautiful, and Be The Blessing. I believe in you.
Momma G*

Sending out vast amounts of gratitude to the courageous voices of Saul Williams, Darren Francis, Margaret Atwood, Ani DiFranco, Andrew Morrison, Leonard Cohen, Lottie Summers, and many other writers who made an imprint on my literary mark. A special shout out to the healers and the helpers; thank you for making the world a safer space. Lastly, Thank you, Javier Rosado and Tiffany Rhoads, for your technical support and editing.

The Crow and A Back Alley

Walking down an alley
a back road in Olympia,
I know this place.

A crow flies overhead
and caws at me.

Two decades pass,
in a different town,
it's the same.
The crow knows my face
and secrets.

A yearning, pulling me in.
It's foggy, ethereal.
Impossible to speak to,
outside of my mind,

spiraling me down,
far away from this town.

Spray-can Street murals,
graffitied on an artist's scene.
Local hipster shops,
specialty coffee spots
and The Childhood's End Gallery
through the fog of
a Pacific Northwest morning.

Urine smells ripe on buildings,
bodies cocooning in tattered
woolen blankets,
plaid, houndstooth,
and multi-colored filthy sleeping bags in an
early morning, cobblestoned alley.

I wander around this town.
I sign petitions and pray.
I focus on underreported news
and greener alternatives.
I wonder and action on Mead's idea
about few people making significant
changes to civilization being viable.

In pale pink,
children float on a smooth,
spotless surface inside this
downtown building.

Tiny ballerinas spinning,
translucent skirts
blurring into a form,
a silhouette.

They are twirling in time,
a little girl's whipped cream dream,
topped with a pink
soft-toed cherry shoe.

I concern myself with abundant recreation
and locating matching socks.

Still, I see the crow flying overhead,
it caws at me.
It follows me to my car.

After all this time,
some things, it seems,
will remain the same.

Girl House

Pink,
Polka dot,
Playful,
Plum berries,
whipping wistful willow trees
in the tropics of a park in St Pete.

Wild Orchids,
an opening that's roots
crumble bark on trees,
as fireflies ride on translucent wings,

as an unfolding,
wrapping,
swarming,
as a falling safe
polka-dot rolling,

spinning,
tumbling,
leaf's spots for cocooning,
amid berries being reborn,
being anew
as a refreshing view
of an old Florida city's landscape.

Women in Black

(Percival landing protest, every
Friday night, Olympia, WA 2008)

Mourning loss and grief in the Middle East,
lives of the innocent,
the unknown taken,
vanished,
lost by angry ideals.
Governments enforcing
aggression, fear, insanity.

I escape to the street in a
black hooded coat
assuming the stance
selected this past year.
I've mastered the art of standing perfectly
still for sixty enormous minutes.

In prayer position,
I imagine someone shooting
me more than the bird,
like Rachel Corrie but an assault rifle,
a crow, and white roses.

If they knew me better,
they'd understand my sadness,
my rage,
and they'd send Peonies,
pale pink in particular.

Though Peonies only bloom
in late spring or early summer.

Planning a fantasy drive-by execution,
according to season,
to favorite flower,
is absurdly complicated.

If I didn't have ridiculously
adorable daughters,
Who knows what I might?

I put on my raincoat,

walk home

and feel slushy

rain hit my face.

Thawing out, I disrobe and transform
into the softest, cotton sleep
shirt in my bottom drawer.
I climb back in bed,
cozy up under the covers
and vanish into a white light
I envision
that surrounds my body.

Woman In Black, Olympia, WA 2006
(Artist Unknown)

Be Still

Columns contort into clouds
that become wings
as my cracked eyelids close.
I wrap my limbs in a downy warmth.

A Florida sunshine seeps through
my cool shade of gray.
A Pacific NW space, my place,
I try to escape from my
mind, hand over heart
beating, ba bam,
bam, bam, bam, quickening.

I want to learn,
to know,
to be still.
Be still, ba bam,
bam, bam, bam, bam.
I turn my palms upward,

open my mind,
moments stand still,
unlike my
heart, a drum.

Clanging, ba, baaa, bam, bam, bam,
switched on,
jangling,
trying to unplug
my emotion of beats and colors
of drums from skins, sweating
off of backs I've never seen.
And stories
circled up as children waiting to
hear something significant
to save their
loss of innocence, their thrive.
What are we all looking for,
peace and pulse,
persisting,
the beat is alive and oversized
badgering my calm.
I lean in and let it rock me to sleep.

Broken Mother

Walking through without you,
I bump into walls,
remember the falls
and wonder how long
it will take me to tie my shoes.

Mother,
Momma,
Mana,
like bread.
Basic, like nourishment,
beginning in the womb.

Wet, warm, shared life,
born,
blessed with a cord,
connected like instilled compassion,
passion for protecting,
detecting the demons on the other side.

The provider of flowers fled,
she didn't have the stamina to stick around.

Preoccupied,
she did not connect the dots.
She did not pick up pieces
of her fractured mirror
wrapped up like a burrito,
I'm borrowing air.
Essential,
unwilling,
fractured,
and broken mother.

Glass

Glass,
my fire,
Like the sun,
a ball of molten mystery,

I reach out to explore its depth,
then withdraw as the heat burns my hand.

Tempted still,
the allure of my wicked mistress.
She sticks out her pump and trips me.

A journey,
I sweat soak my skin,
burn under my flesh,
and break from the furnace
in a Florida dress.

Evening arrives,
warm and powdery white sand
on an unexplored beach,
the sun descends with
a palette of baby blue blending
into a flamingo coast.

Calling my attention,
I knot up my cobalt sleeveless
sundress and savor in the silky,
warm sensations under my feet.
Tasting misted salted drops,
air cooling my cheeks,
my hair blowing wildly,
a welcome,
a light,
a bliss and a home in this nearly
perfect day.

Memories of Jenny

She left,
lingering her lit energy,
freckled face,
fearless laugh and the deep
red hue of her fingernails.

Cozy, clean clothing lines,
Mixed matched chairs,
as if, no cares.

a Winnie the Pooh comfortability,
she and me,
mountains of giggles
and uncertainty.

Hand in Hodgkins,
dripping,
glowing,

burning,
fiery,
stuck, struck,
seeping into her circulatory,

traveling,
consuming,
competing,
winning,
for now.

Until and after the world bends, burns and
illuminates, I will miss you
madly.

Great Big Tongue Slide

(Life before motherhood)

He opens his mouth and
I am going for a ride,
a great big tongue slide.

Down his throat,
slipping,
swimming,
back peddling,

weaving,
sorting through,
deeper down.

Deeper down,
deeper down to the bile,

to the organs,
to the obstacles
that confront me.

I jump rope
his intestines,
swan dive his sperm,
my pet fish.

He's afraid,
my insatiable truth,
looks to his clock,
hoping my games stop.

Blood Seeped Borders

I am immobilized while
my laptop won't power up.
Panic penetrating my pores.

Will my penmanship even be legible?

The technological age is here,
it conquered nature.

Minds are numb
to notions of global warming.

Apathy consumes civilization.

Succulent designer chocolate,
Juicy bling bags
soon paid for with crypto are
fogging our foundation.

G-d gets mad at our society,
blacking out cities
with a scientific vengeance
and religious hypocrisy.

Catastrophic natural and
intentional disasters intensify.

Tsunamis blanketing coasts
while fires and hurricanes
wipe slates, states, F.E.M.A. clean?

Remains of fresh naked
territories, exposed.
Maybe we are not so civilized after all?

Meanwhile, the Dalai Lama visits Seattle,
and the freeway
becomes a parking lot.

People protest,
pray for peace,
The US bombs Iraq.

Blood seeps borders
staining our soul.

PattiZILLA

She was fine at 45,
hard not to stare.
Jet black hair and green piercing eyes,
Patricia, at center stage.

Then, her wedding ceremony and
she bloomed past perfection.
How he bloomed her to wilt.

And her hair and makeup,
as glam as it gets, were fast manifesting
PattiZILLA.

I am awake with her till 3:00 A.M.
the night before her wedding.
Later today, she will marry a man
who watches marathons of The
Beverly Hillbillies.

If I was different,
I might find that endearing;
I'm not.

If I thought he was charming,
generous,
If I thought he'd make my girl smile
or feel newly wedded,
I could overlook the fleet of red flags
sailing toward us late that night.

He evoked a feeling,
the chills.
The hair stood up on the back of my neck.
I was confident we were in trouble.

Instead of speaking out
and shaking her straight,
I looked over and noticed
her long stem red roses and froze.

Valentine's Day,
A commercially scheduled love day.
Divine store-bought sparkly jewels,
fragrant bouquets,

specialty chocolates and
dinner reservations.

Despite all the contrived commercialism,
I fall for the flash,
The flavors
and the FTD disturbances.

Her red roses,
on her vanity,
Placed precisely
next to photos of her family.

She brought me over a single red rose.
I placed it in a charming yet
masterfully blown sandblasted bud vase.

And my vase,
my single red rose
my gloom of her sailing away
blindfolded into red-flagged marriage,
so stunning,
I forgot my client was waiting in the lobby.

PattyZilla
Painting 36"x36" by Greer Sommer

Breathing forest

I wait like a breathing forest to be walked in,
crunching colored leaves in
a still morning's dew.

Droplets of a dawn's early walk
wet my thirst, chill my bones,
remind me
I'm a long way from home.

I wait for the warmth,
the sun,
a moment,
as if I'm a spectator in it.

Stuck in the lights,
frozen,
many times,
pressing buttons,
distractions,

killing time.
Needing to get away from my mind.
Do I crash or do I sprint away?

Exhaling into the infinity of
a Pacific NW winter
and a wonderland I have yet to embrace,
I wait to walk amongst the enormous
forested trees, with you or alone,
my beloved stranger,
comfortably.

A Memory and Meditation of Naranja Lakes

My head on your heart,
a cradle,
rocking back and forth
to Naranja Lakes.

Sunshine in my skies,
I remember smiles
pure like pink clouds,
comforting me with simplicity,
floating on seven orange lakes,
contentedly.

Bringing me home to a comfortability.
A joy in me,
eternity?
Yes, I believe in divinity,
like infinity.

Sparkling stars and
sky willing me,
to my eventuality, hum?

Ooommmmmmmmmmmmmmmmmmm ~

Grandma's Room

I'm flying on pure adrenaline
like the turbulent flight that takes me there.

I'm reflecting on Grandma's familiar smells,
a place of cigarettes and Channel #5,
of melodramatic scanting
of four females,
biting their tongues,
being diplomatic.

Back to a draining repose,
a caution
that does not tear fresh wounds
out of healed scars.

And as we fly there,
we are eating our peanuts
and forgetting our lives

and our pilot's aggressive
take-off is nothing
we can control.

And when we arrive,
a discernible odor and fatal fog will hit me
like being trapped in a burning building.

The stench of something like,
"I wish I were already
underground with grandpa."

Words from her mouth like
rotten well water.

I want to scream,
to jolt her out of her narcissism,
just for the moment
long enough to acknowledge her
three granddaughters before her.

Instead, I think of her three-
mile morning walks,
the thousands of dollars
she spent to remove her wrinkles.

How she believed with conviction,
"When I took off my gloves,
everybody took off their gloves."

She's made it past the last
stage of death and dying.
She'll never pass denial or despair.
I wish I knew what to say
to clear the air.

Everyone around me is busying themselves
with Skymall magazines and
the latest Hollywood fads.

No one seems to notice what's
outside those windows.

Those Three Words

You ask what's on my mind.
I say the train.
I think that's a caboose.
Remember, like the one we saw
last week?

La musicale', of brass and steel,
waver of the wand,
weaver of sound.

Train and conductor,
circular missed connections of
metal on metal on tracks
like a rise and flow
diverting in the middle.

I give you these words,
these three words in a mailbag.

Much safer on the tracks as
it makes its way past.

I say them three times in a row,
in my mind
as the train grabs hold.
And I like the sound of that triple set,
the three:

As body,
as mind
as spirit,
The Trinity.

Like tickets to a symphony,
when I leave that train,
when you won't think I'm driving too fast.

Those three words:
circulate,
penetrate,
permeate my cells,
my circulatory,
my being.

Those three small words,
and now,
they've grown:
and now they're huge,
and now,
gigantic,
gi-normous,
galactic.

Like moon,
like planets,
like stars,

The sun
and sky,
the earth,
la Luna,
mi amour.

Like Counting Cars,
I'm counting boxcars.

I wait to cross over those tracks,
to say those words
each time I look at you.

As petals in a translucent bowl,
in a giant bathtub for two.
As those blooms,
I've opened,
unfolded,
fallen onto a table
like a feast with secret ingredients.

Putting petals in my bathwater,
smiles in my pocket,
to swim in
to soak in
as our train approaches,
as I pour a perfectly steeped
cup of Hibiscus tea.

Soaking Epsom salt for aches
and heated wants,
wishes with folioles floating
as pink stringed sounds,
arising iridescent bubbles, a
fusion of sultry winds,
immersed in an aroma of
coconut and gardenia,
permeating,
sinking into the heat.

Orchestrated,
accompanied,
those three words
that may endure this hot water,

unable to fully cross,
to completely relax,

tied to the tracks
as the train approaches fast

Tug-O-War and Me

....

Lingering in the peripheral,
words, screenshots, and selfies
that flash before my mind.

Bleeps, beeps, and "oh my" notifications.

I balance on two red woven rafts,
one, under each foot,

I ride upon a reflection of you and I,
a tsunami, in my mind?

I am surfing on uncertainty
and brackish waters,
ambiguous signs of sunlight ahead.

I proceed to the night.

I combined ancient yogic postures
with Jedi mind beams.

I bent, willowed, and wavered
risking my raw and vulnerable heart,
I collected sadness like coins,
placing them in a satin satchel,
stashed away in the top drawer,
hidden on a brackish island.

Life is
dripping,
overflowing,
into a metal bowl,
left outside
to weather then rust.

Tears flow plentifully
while caravans immigrate
from barren harvests
of beans, soy, and corn.
I plant and chant,
"food not bombs",
wake and
nothing changed.

So, I sit cross-legged
and look to the stars.
I sit in hope.
I sit in fear,
In despair,
I sit fairly near
yet seemingly solar systems,
and galaxies away.

I see your light
and notice my awakening.

Where could I go from here?

It's clear.
I have exposed my flesh,
I have taken out my bones.

One by one,
I held each bone
cautiously,
Inquisitively,
attentively

I place them on the only silver platter I own.

I inspect each bone,
this may be the last time I hold my bones.

Grooves and elevations,
imperfections and failed attempts,
chipped away,
eroded with crashed cars,
fractured,
broken bones, bicycles, clamped,
strong and frail
co-existing.

Loved as lived,
aged in time,
eroding but alluringly written rhymes.
warn as my favorite platform
Doc Martin Mary Janes.

A star shoots up and outward
in a glowing diagonal direction.
RocketZilla
I made a wish.

Illuminated dust sparkling,
disappearing in the night sky.

Out of the sum,
one hundred thousand million
stars in a milky way.
I see you shine.
I soak in your light.
Magnetized to your spark,
illuminated by your galaxy.

I keep a distance of light-years away.

Me, safe, in this space,
immersed in stars,
caught in a commute,
trying to stay off the
definitive crossed lines
that may blur
and sometimes wiggle
where I wean, then vanish as
I ponder my next move.

Happy Birthday
Mychele

White and yellow daisies grace
my dining room table.

A lingering gentle bouquet lasting
longer than Mychele and Jim's
relationship.

There is something so beautiful and
feminine about white daisies and Mychele.

Today is Mychele's birthday.

She will smile her joker's mouth
and laugh her cartoon cackle.

She will nearly convince me
she's unaffected
from last week's lack of sleep.

So, Jim, next time you go
around giving daisies,
I'd recommend saving your pennies
for a dozen pale pink roses.

You can be sure they will unfold brilliantly
within forty-eight hours,
then die by the time your skin leaves
with its lingering effects
on someone's flesh.

Jim, you lost the brightest star in the sky.

Mychele, hold tight,
We'll make it right,
your night,
sweet friend,
Shine bright, pure white light.

Kiss Off

Used to be a hot tamale
homecoming princess,
now hidden in a crowd avoiding a gaze
because those eyes remind me of him.
And the anger left holes in my heart.

I close the cage.
Love bird plucking its feathers.

Emptiness erodes an appetite for life.
I am waiting for hunger to hit.

Lost in rows of cemetery stones
an angel cries near concrete tombs,
over losses
never attempted, to wake up
day ends
poof.

I open a book called Kiss-Off and fall in love.
The first page: a chorus of the band,
Violent Femmes song, Kiss Off:

"For Everything, Everything,
Everything, Everything!"

A child sits across from me and
picks up a book on my table.

He asks me what I want to
be when I grow up.

I give him a confused,
tilted head, odd glance and responded:
not old,
slow,
crumbling,
waiting for the next disaster,
sick of
all the smiles and giggles around me.

The happiness leaves his eyes.

This, too, will 'go down on
your permanent record',

Out,
the parking lot,
home sweet safe
Cozy under the covers...

Abandoned youth,
wanting it whether.

The Dissolution

I wore a cheerful shade of red on my
mouth to mourn seven years' wed.
Done, dead
like a Hollywood film, he fled.

Led,
betrayed,
disrespected.

Consumed by the fear of me,
depression.

Two daughters, so young, so sad,
what could I have done?

NO,
It's done!

Civilization selected the
disposable wedding.

We can have it with fries and a plastic toy.

A toy that will break when
we accidentally crush
it with black boots.

Under his big step,
crushed,
soul impenetrable.

Saul Williams on a Saturday Night

(Dedicated to an extraordinary poet,
inspired by and for Saul Williams)

I have to say,
Your light nearly blinded me
and I'm Stu, Stu,
stuttering
all over myself,
talking to you.

So please pardon a schoolgirl version of me,
as I follow the sparks on a walk,
your rhyme,
changing the trajectory of mind, divine.

He smiled and laughed with
love and generosity
so as not to generate a
hes-it-at-ion or stall in me
or my call...ing?

Ring, Ring?

Saul, you spoke to me so simply,
I could breathe better,
my pulse, it slowed.

Like an exhaled moment,
sitting down at the doctor's office
with just one minute to spare
after an afternoon of head-spinning,
traffic jamming, Verizon
Wireless negotiating,
and my child has another detention.
And that's how I arrived and found you.
Nothing less than magical fairy dust,
from China, Penny, wise,
sublime,
and stellar in her constellations,
led me to you with a whisper
and a Shhhhhh.

Appearing with a carafe of water,
Penny saw I needed some:

'G-d, Buddha, Malcolm, Yahweh.
Deepak, Pope Francis, Jesus, Tolle,
Ruiz, Redfield, Mother Teresa,'
and probably some of Bob Geldof,
but that was decades ago,
and besides,
he was brilliantly attached.

Penny provided me with a
secret suite number
and made me swear
not to share
where or with
anyone else
besides one radio equipment operator.

After all, she said,
you spin his rhymes more than
any others' combined,
so come on, follow me, I will lead you there.

BOOM,
BANG,
BEYOND!

sometimes my life amazes me,
stupendously,
serendipitously,
spectacularly,
and I have to
Praise the Lord.

We recognized it was the
birth of Malcolm X,
discussed mutual appreciation,
transformation
and letting go of fear.

Climbing the edges of a cardboard box,
breaking down borders with diagonal lines,
Rocket Zilla,
shooting up and out
anytime the mind and soul will let go of,
go,

Go, GO,

Transcend, I said!

Resisting my mind,
dismissing what he said about me.
I will shine,
despite not feeling so fine.

I continue to build a belief in
me and Yahweh.
Hear my thanks for your glow,
dear Saul,
I just wanted you to know,

I satiate with your rhythm,
the magical generosity of your time
and your solutions
about fear
regarding bravery and beyond.

Peace and prosper,
continue to grow
and glow
and show the world
that men can be soft,
soulful and poetically moving,
evoking a shift, realigning a mind,

a spark, electricity,
the momentum
opening minds,
over generations,
changing times.

(DJ Diagonal)

Yom Kippur

Yom Kippur service
packed with people
for the Day of Atonement.

It is Fall's cleansing from a
Gregorian October introspection.

I wear black and white,
half heathen, half pure, unsure?

Look inward and ask for forgiveness,
for wrongdoings,
wear white for rebirth
and purity.

Rabbi Seth with a poem from Maya Angelou
and the connection,
the historical consideration,
my tears' source?

My response to fear is to interfere,
an obligation for Jewish people.
The protest, the protection,
the pay attention
to those of less fortunate.

On Talmud teachings,
Rabbis reside only in towns
where charitable services take place.

I weep when I hear the rabbi talk
about repairing the world.

Don't be satisfied with people being hungry.
'Hear the calls, their hurts, their wounds or
be punished for
transgressions of the world.'

The gates are closing.
I'm wondering.

Secret Snake Eyes

Hiding behind black-rimmed
iridescent shades,
a smirky reptilian glance becomes
a complicated circumstance.

Work events,
duties flashing before my eyes.
A friendly smile,
took a walk, shared a smoke,
omitting unmentionables.

I am in danger,
but I am walking.

I feel my heart pounding,
solid,
a bass drum,

heavy my limbs,
accelerating, my heart.

Everything is hazy.
I can't seem to speak.
I can't move my limbs.
I detest you as you represent
everything that becomes agony.

I am surviving.
My heart is beating,
pounding.

I am breathing.
I am slaying my dragon,
listening to my wisdom.

I am locating my center.
I am finding my thoughts,
I am clutching my power in a firm fist.

I am here,
home with me.
I'm aware.

I Am Mighty.

May 23 and my Goldfish

It's May 23, the anniversary, gone, dead.

The bliss, the kiss...

till death do us part.

All I wanted was the Goldfish.

It's May 23 and my marriage is
dead along with my Goldfish.

Finished, flushed down the toilet
like the vows and commitment.

I swim around in my mind
like a swirl in the bowl.
I question the pollution I put into
the bowl, my marriage?

Sadly, my finned friends died
instead of thrived.
I wonder if I should keep the tank?

Tiny treasures,
memories tucked away in my hand,
thrown in the tank like a wishing well,
a better place.

An idyllic life,
tossing glass stones,
translucent shells,
shards of sparkles

intentionally thrown in a tank.

Collected,
cleaned,
swished around in my hands

as I hold them
on the anniversary
of our birth and death
of our life together.

Motherhood Fills Me

The walk has become a
tiptoe of many years.
Trying to love me because you
couldn't remember you did.
Duties of motherhood fill me.

Picking up pieces of pink houses
and rearranging Lego lands,

I cook their favorite Friday night meal
and light a single candle.

I trade in those sexy slip-on shoes
for diapers, wipes, and wet-eyed kisses.

I stack,
pack,
fold and pray.

Wonder about going away.

Get out,
get moving
where I'm far from the aggression,
repression and
rivers of self-ridicule.

And the loneliness
rides up on me like a wave,
pummeling me high tide
I stand firmly in a puddle of pollution.

Not wanting to waste time
or lose my mind,
I let you go.
I set you free.

The duties of motherhood fill me.

I still feel an occasional amount of might,
despite the spit-up and drool
on the back of my blouse.

How else can we be strong?

How else can we be blessed?

So, we say yes,
opening a buried box of beloved,
brilliant colors and rainbows.

Just hold tight,
Junie B. Jones' and The Yucky,
Blucky, Fruitcake tonight.

I smile to myself as I continue to
read past the point where Sonya
and Romy are fast asleep.

I won't tell them what happens to the
Yucky, Blucky, Fruitcake.

White of Winter

Seeking out light in the white of winter.

I find comfort in a friend
and a cup of chamomile.

A place to locate our hearts.

Lost within an infinite number
of smooth stones,
buried in a rushing river,
somewhere,
lost,
off the map.

A treasure?
A fresh, raw
throbbing wound.

Pain softened by sounds, and smiles of
children's giggles paired with
Russian Tea Cakes.
Dressing Polly Pockets
and spilling grape juice on a spectacular,
round floral rug.

Can you imagine the kind of friend
whose expression never changed?

Making memories,
bringing in the new year with you Monica,
exactly where I want to be.

Art of Noise

A new genre?

Scratchy, distorted sounds
from a disc jockey.

Blue hair spilling out sex appeal
over the population played. Spinning sounds
like power tools, scratching and grating.

Torn jeans with a hue of baby blue eyes.
Metro, Pan, Bi, Poly, Trans, two-spirited,

ABCDEFG, oozing out all over
him, me, any and everyone.

Audience beyond the dope dealt,
and I'm trying not to berate.

Yet, those dimples.
Superficial society dove right
in, feeding a vampy,
trampy ooze-o-meter, not a metaphor?
Call me square; I don't care.

My man isn't mine, and that will be fine.
Fear, despair, and what will I dare?
I slip away.

I wonder where my windy limbs willow.
Like a vine,
I hope I climb, a new space
a better place, expect to
walk through a gate,
wanting to elevate,
an unknown sight,
a doorway,
lead me right,
let there be light.

Diagonal In My Sleep

Tenacity like a toothache,
she plugs away.

Fragmented fears flicker
subconscious projections of
faint translucent film squares.

Images flying by so quickly,
they're undetectable.
I get hunches though still not certain?

My dreams know and push me around.
A dark brunette daring for something more:

divine,
refined,
emotionally benign,
maybe even sublime?

Balancing more than I can manage,
in my sleep,
I mash away at the enamel in my mouth,
grinding fears,
failures and
new beginnings.

A boulder bouncing off the back
of the blue pickup bed,
creating a new
form.

I read alone in my bed.
I'm waiting to move over to the other side.
Seven years of marriage
structured my sleep.
I begin to move my leg
diagonally to break out.
I'm dipping my toe into the puddle;
it may prove toxic and poison me.

I decide to stretch my mind,
create a baseline.
I write it all down,
needing solitude.

I light a candle.
Then, I light a fire.
I burn away the sadness, struggle,
the hurt and suffering,
smoldering before my eyes,
mesmerized by the flame.

I watch the smoky pages
become indecipherable,
letters and photos burning,
curling,
emulsions marbling on caustic paper.

I breathe away an enormous burden
and an exhaustive exhalation~

Wipe my feet of aches and wishes,
wants and anguish.
Letting go of,
feeling lighter,
stretching diagonally,
both legs in my bed.

Big Black Boots
Painting by Greer Sommer

Any Minute Now

The sand in the hourglass slips through,
slowly;
I am six,
waiting for my birthday cake,
another candle,
again,
now it's eight.

Each night I ask,
how many days?
You say,
31 days to go,
and I know that time is creeping,
crawling,
yet, I watch the clock:
tick, tock, tick tock, tick tock.

It's 10 now 12,
and I wonder,
will I be a queen
or the ogre?

I wait,
I wonder.

Will you notice my hair,
my flare,
will I feel the up and down stare?

I hope you won't care;
that's why I might dare.

It's a few days away,
I am full of delight.
I'm holding tight...

tick tock,
tick tock,
tick tock~

As soon as the sand falls slowly
through the hourglass.

Inauguration Day

Refresh the view.
In perspective, new.
In nature,
preserve.
In a community,
serve.
In global responsibility,
observe.

A new dawn,
a new day.
An invigorated nation,
come forth today.

For all who dare,
A task is here.

You are all invited
to come and share.
Do you still care?

We... In This Together
Artwork by Greer Sommer

Ode to Death
Do Us Part

In Hebrew, the number seven is called Shiva.
Jewish people are to mourn the passing
of their loved ones for seven
days.

The Hebrew Talmud declares that
'seven days of rejoicing after marriage
(Sheva Berachot), so too he enacted
seven days of mourning' (Shiva).

You are dead to me.
I completed the ritual.

I reach into my head,
and I grab a chunk of hair.
I wasn't aware,
But NO,
I no longer do that.

I begin to section off
three, equal,
small chunks of hair,
partitioned into a tiny slice
of a micro braid.

I know you don't like it when
I wear my hair like that.

It reminds you of our ghetto school,
how we were integrated.
How everyone and everything
was wild and uncontrollable,
like me,
apparently

and ironically,
your kinky hair.

Following a cemetery burial,
Jewish people cover mirrors,
wear black
and tear a piece of clothing.
Kriah, a Hebrew word meaning "tearing."

Modern Jews frequently wear
a small black ribbon
over their hearts.

I don't support that sweet sentiment.
I ripped up the sexy black
dress you bought me
and wrapped it around
my arm.

A Black Mamba
from the African Sub-Saharan,
large and venomous,
poisoning my brain.
Dendroaspis polylepis,
complicated and scientific as facts
you are disinterested in accepting.
Facts that used to live in a nonnegotiable
land of the free and the brave.

At least you praise the Lord.
And why can't you comprehend
we can have it both ways?
Why wouldn't it all compute, align,
symbiotically and not necessarily in

harmony, as we are told to anticipate,
anyway?

I tried to sparkle,
but that look of disapproval.
It clicked the lock on my prison cage.

I clung to the bars.
I will never be beige enough
despite trying till I'm...

Grandpa told me we could
not go to the carnival
or do anything fun because Bubby died.

No vain activities,
like selfies,
lipstick,
bling on my shoes or my
'nails that shine like justice.'

Nothing fun like bubble gum
or shiny barrettes.

I am walking behind Carolyn Smith
lost in her cornrows of headsquares,

barrettes, and giggly loud,
lip glossed girls.

Levi corduroys and ponytailed teens
transform into puffy,
white marshmallow
uniformed gym suits.

Girls in the locker room,
dancing on benches,
singing and sporting their OMG,
exposed boobs,
so liberating and free.

I do my best to avoid eye contact.
I change my shirt,
exposing my bra, swiftly.

The dancing girls' flow,
combined
rhythmic time,
like wavy raked sandy lines
and a rare exotic confidence
never seen.

Braids like native lands,
organic corn and sweet
non-GMO carrots,
lined up
in formation ready, like the Christmas
tree farms and pine scents
in our Decembers.

Just as succulent Valentines
in perfect 1" squares,
divided, sectioned,
I tried to stay
in your perfectly fancy
and freshly Fabreezed lines.

For Shiva,
people come to my grandparent's house
bringing trays of intuitive family recipes,
smoked salmon,
cream cheese,
everything bagels,
knishes and kugel,
just a few.

Pastries of rugelach,
macaroons, roasted nuts

and marbled pound cakes,
magically appearing,
delivered, several times a day,

wrapped up
in a domestic
sexual servant package,

with a smile,
all the while.

You wanted a diluted version of me,
a grayer shade
where I'm not dancing freely on the island,
or being noticed.

Where you kept me 30 feet away from
those island men and I never even cared,
only that you dared.

Not Stepford enough,
you ask me to submit,
so bank, beige manager,
why did you marry a colorful me?

I excused your behavior
as my poor ego boundaries
begged to be
imprisoned,
even by your wrath.

Men dressed in black
circled up
in my grandparent's living room.
They're praying in Hebrew, looking
like orthodox rabbis.

Ladies roam about
unpacking bakery boxes
of black and white cookies,
jelly bars and a variety of
small specialty cake squares.

Men continue to pray.
Ladies cry and catch up.

Children weave in and out of the kitchen
toward the back patio
where they are huddled
around my stray cat, Snowball.

Platters of egg salad,
chopped liver,
whitefish salad,
and deli meats, are
served with Gefilte Fish
and horseradish.

It's been 779 days since you
removed yourself from "us",
with that cold stare.

So chilly,
I still get goosebumps
even, when the sun is out.

And it's always out
because I live in Florida
where you left me,
a jagged silver stab,
post-surgeries.

I needed a safe space,
your hand,
a polishing cloth to shine.

I'm traveling on grief highway
doing donuts
instead of eating them.

Though sometimes,
I still feel a choking in my throat
when I think of you.

It's a grief symptom
that occurs when I don't say
what's heaviest on my
mind.

So, I will reach into my head;
I will pull a chunk of hair aside,
sectioning off three equal strands,
I begin to weave the sections of hair
into my memory.

Lines and rows,
sweet strawberries at Knott's berry farm,
braids like seeds and smiles
as integrated kids
skip rope,
long lines and laughs at lunch,
rows like veins

full of blood,
full of life,

veins reaching upward
toward my heart.
From my heart
to my rhyme,

braids taking me back
a time,
when I didn't care
about eye contact,
passionate kisses or
being asked about my day.

Thus, I travel in my imagination,

going,
flowing,
and glowing about the future,
the freed up,
the island,
my dreams.

My hope,
created,

in small increments,
then doubt,
and finally,
the death of us.

Why did I allow you to mistreat me,
repeatedly?

I need to look at me
emotionally,
setting limits
on how people
behave toward me.

I will hold on to my divinity,
what's left of my dignity
and seek
to forgive both of us
for breaking my heart.

Now, the wind carries me,
with songs and sparkles,
colors to captivate my attention span.

I dip my fingers into hues and places
I would have never

Imagined.

I'm flowing,
growing,
thriving,
and flying
into the ethereal.

Light years away
with the light and stars,
I may go to Mars
or my own kind of
paradise.
Where brilliant shades of cerulean,
magenta,
periwinkle
and chartreuse
captivate my ability
to transform a canvas.
change a life,
elicit a spark
and find meaning in,
An Infinite Web

~The End

P.T.S.D. Growth
Artwork by Greer Sommer